Earth-Friendly Crafts in **5** Easy Steps

Earth-Friendly Christmas Crafts in 5 Easy Steps

Anna Llimós

Enslow Elementary

an imprint of

Enslow Publishers, Inc.

40 Industrial Road
Box 398
Berkeley Heights, NJ 07922
USA

http://www.enslow.com

Note to Kids and Parents: Getting earth-friendly materials is easy to do. Just look around your house for containers, wrappers, and other things you would throw out. Some of these recyclable materials may include plastic, paper, cardboard, cork, and cloth. The materials used in this book are suggestions. If you do not have an item, use something similar. Use any color material and paint that you wish. Use your imagination!

Safety Note: Be sure to ask for help from an adult, if needed, to complete these crafts.

Enslow Elementary, an imprint of Enslow Publishers, Inc.

Enslow Elementary® is a registered trademark of Enslow Publishers, Inc.

English edition copyright © 2014 by Enslow Publishers, Inc.

Translated from the Spanish edition by Stacey Juana Pontoriero.
Edited and produced by Enslow Publishers, Inc.

Library of Congress Cataloging-in-Publication Data
Llimós Plomer, Anna.
  [Navidad (2006). English]
  Earth-friendly Christmas crafts in 5 easy steps / Anna Llimós.
       pages cm — (Earth-friendly crafts in 5 easy steps)
  Translation of: Navidad / Anna Llimós. — Barcelona : Parramón Paidotribo, 2006.
  Includes bibliographical references and index.
  Summary: "Provides step-by-step instructions on how to create fourteen simple Christmas crafts using various materials"—Provided by publisher.
  ISBN 978-0-7660-4188-2
  1. Christmas decorations—Juvenile literature. 2. Handicraft—Juvenile literature.
  3. Salvage (Waste)—Juvenile literature. I. Title.
  TT900.C4L59413 2013
  745.594'12—dc23
                            2012013291

Future edition:
MAR 2 8 2014
Paperback ISBN 978-1-4644-0307-1

Originally published in Spanish under the title *Navidad*.
Copyright © 2006 Parramón Paidotribo-World Rights
Published by Parramón Paidotribo, S.L., Badalona, Spain

Production: Sagrafic, S.L.
Text: Anna Llimós
Illustrator: Nos & Soto

Printed in Spain
112012 Indice, S.L., Barcelona, Spain
10 9 8 7 6 5 4 3 2 1

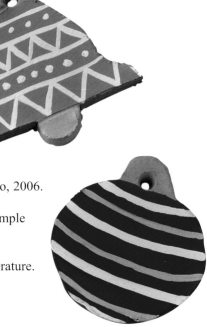

Contents

Place Card Clips

MATERIALS

3 clip-style wooden clothespins
paint—different colors
paintbrush
air-drying clay
toothpick
card stock
scissors
white glue

1 Paint each clothespin any way you wish. Let dry.

2 Mold two small balls and two leaves out of clay. You can use a toothpick to create the veins on the leaves. Let dry.

3 Mold a small Christmas tree out of clay. Let dry.

4 Mold Santa Claus's head out of clay. Let dry.

5 Cut card stock into rectangles. Glue the clay figures onto the clothespins. Let dry.

Write your friends' and family's names on them.

Angel

MATERIALS

toilet tissue tube
permanent black marker
scissors
paint-different colors
paintbrush
felt
white glue
cotton

1 Draw an angel on the toilet tissue tube. The body goes on the front, and the wings go on the back.

2 Cut out the angel along the drawn lines.

3 Paint the head and body. Let dry.

6

4 Paint the wings. Decorate the clothes any way you wish. Let dry.

5 For the hair, cut some felt and glue it onto the head. Let dry. Draw the eyes, nose, and mouth. Glue some cotton underneath the angel to make clouds.

What a lovely angel!

Ornaments

1 Cut a bunch of squares from tissue paper. Mix water and glue in a plastic bowl to make gluewash.

2 Brush gluewash over the pieces of tissue paper to stick them onto the Styrofoam balls.

3 Mold small cones out of clay. Glue them to the balls. Let dry.

8

4 Stick a paper clip into each clay cone while it is still soft. Let the cones harden.

5 Tie a piece of raffia around each paper clip.

Hang them on your tree!

Greeting Cards

MATERIALS

card stock-different colors
scissors
white glue
corrugated cardboard-different colors

1 Cut a rectangle from a piece of card stock. Fold it.

2 On the inside, glue a rectangle from different colored card stock.

3 Draw stars or any other shape on the backs of different colored pieces of corrugated cardboard. Cut them out.

4 Glue the stars onto the front of the card.

5 For a cool design, you can glue only half of the star onto the front so the other half hangs over the edge. You can design many different cards.

Give them to your friends!

Wrapping Paper

MATERIALS

Styrofoam™ sheet
scissors
black permanent marker
pencil
corks
white glue
paint
paintbrush
wrapping paper

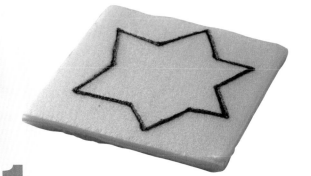

1 Cut a square from the Styrofoam sheet. Draw a star or any other shape you want with a black permanent marker. Trace the shape over with pencil, pressing down hard enough to leave an impression.

2 Glue a cork to the back of the square. Let dry. This is your stamp.

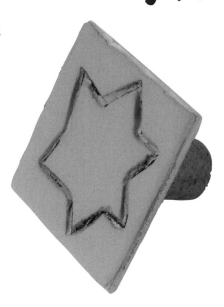

3 Cover the stamp in paint.

4 Stamp the wrapping paper. Make sure to press down hard enough to leave a sharp, clear design. Let it dry.

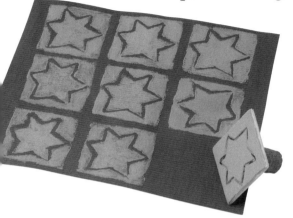

5 You can use all different shapes and colors to create festive designs.

Wrap your gifts.

Reindeer and Sleigh

MATERIALS

card stock–light brown and dark brown
black permanent marker
scissors
white glue
colored pencils
2 clip-style wooden clothespins
corrugated cardboard
yarn

1 Draw the reindeer's body on light brown card stock and the antlers on dark brown card stock. Cut them out.

2 Glue the antlers to the head. Let dry. Use colored pencils to add the eyes, nose, and ears.

3 For the legs, attach the two clothespins to the body. For the hooves, cut two pieces of dark brown card stock and glue them to the clothespins.

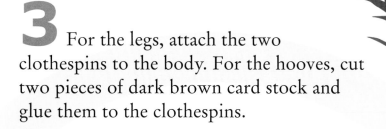

4 Draw the sleigh's two sides and base on corrugated cardboard. Cut them out.

5 Glue the three pieces of the sleigh together. Let dry. Use yarn to tie the sleigh to the reindeer.

Ready to help Santa Claus!

Decorations

MATERIALS

air-drying clay
rolling pin
toothpick
plastic knife
paint-different colors
paintbrush
old toothbrush
ribbon-different colors

1 Use a rolling pin to flatten out a piece of clay. Use the toothpick to sketch shapes into the clay: tree, bell, heart, ornament, and star.

2 Cut the shapes out with the plastic knife.

3 Use the toothpick to make a hole at the top of each shape. Let them dry.

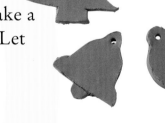

16

4 Paint the shapes. Let dry.

5 Add details. For a speckled look, you can use the old toothbrush to flick paint onto the shapes if you wish. Let dry. Pass a piece of ribbon through each hole.

Decorate your gifts!

Santa Card Holder

MATERIALS

felt-red, white, black, and pink
scissors
cotton
white glue
clip-style wooden clothespins
paint-different colors
paintbrush

1 For Santa's body, cut a strip from red felt. Cut a pair of boots the same width as the body from black felt.

2 Create his face by gluing pieces of felt together. Glue cotton for his hair and beard. Let dry.

3 Glue the face and boots to the strip of red felt. Let dry.

4 Make a hat from red and white felt. Glue it to the head. Let dry.

5 Paint the clothespins and let dry. Fasten the clothespins to the Santa.

Hang all your cards!

19

Christmas Tree

1 Draw and cut out two trees from card stock. On one of the trees, cut a slit from the top to the center. On the other tree, cut a slit from the trunk to the center.

MATERIALS

pencil
green card stock
scissors
cork sheet
white glue
felt—different colors

2 Join the two trees together by slipping one tree into the slit of the other.

3 For the trunk, glue eight small rectangles of cork sheet to the bottom of the tree. Let dry.

4 Cut decorations out of different colored felt. Glue them to the tree and let dry.

5 If you wish, you can make a bow out of a long strip of felt and glue it to the top of the tree.

What a beautiful tree!

Garland

MATERIALS

card stock-different colors
ruler
pencil
scissors
white glue
raffia-2 different colors

1 Use a ruler to draw a straight line on two pieces of card stock. Cut two strips of card stock the same size. Glue one end of each strip together. Let dry.

2 To create a star, start folding the strips over each other in an alternating pattern.

3 Keep folding them until you reach the ends.

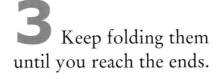

4 Glue the ends together and let dry. You can make many stars using different colors.

5 Cut a piece of raffia from two different colors. Slide the raffia through the stars.

Decorate with the colorful garland.

Flowerpot Stake

MATERIALS

card stock–different colors
black permanent marker
scissors
colored pencils
white glue
raffia
wooden dowel
tape

1 Draw clothes and a hat on card stock with black permanent marker. Cut them out.

2 Cut two legs from card stock. Decorate the hat, clothes, and legs with colored pencils.

3 Cut out a head and two hands from card stock. Draw the face.

24

4 Glue all the parts together. For the hair, glue some raffia on the head. Glue the hat over the hair. Let dry.

5 Tape the wooden dowel to the back of the paper figure.

Stick it in a flowerpot to give it extra holiday cheer!

Winter Scene

MATERIALS

card stock–different colors
scissors
white glue
corrugated cardboard
air-drying clay–different colors
plastic knife

1 Cut out houses and doors from different colored card stock. Glue them to a big sheet of card stock. Let dry.

2 For the roofs, cut out a piece of corrugated cardboard and glue it on. Let dry.

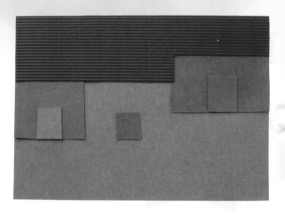

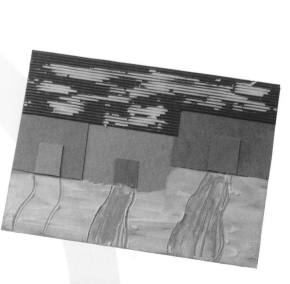

3 Smear white clay on the roofs for snow. Cover the bottom with white clay. Use the plastic knife to scrape out the walkways.

4 To make the snowman, stick two round pieces of clay onto the scene. Make the eyes from two tiny pieces of clay. Add clay snowflakes.

5 Add a nose, hat, buttons, and scarf from clay. Let it dry and harden. Glue the winter scene onto a bigger sheet of card stock.

Hang it in your room!

Little Bells

MATERIALS

egg carton
scissors
toothpick
paint-different colors
paintbrush
old toothbrush
jingle bells
ribbon

1 Cut out three cups from an egg carton. Use the toothpick to poke a hole through each cup.

2 Paint the cups and let dry.

3 Decorate the cups as you wish. You can create a speckled look by using an old toothbrush to flick paint onto them.

4 Tie a jingle bell to one end of the ribbon. Pass the ribbon through one of the cups.

5 Tie another jingle bell onto the same ribbon. Pass the ribbon through another cup. Repeat the same steps with the last jingle bell and cup. Add as many bells as you want!

What wonderful bells!

Shooting Star

1 Draw a star and tail on card stock with black permanent marker. Cut them out.

MATERIALS

card stock
black permanent marker
scissors
colored pencils
white glue
tape
cord

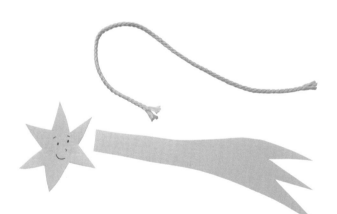

2 Draw a face on the star with colored pencils. Glue the star to the tail. Let dry. Glue or tape the cord to the back of the shooting star.

3 On another piece of card stock, draw a person and cut it out.

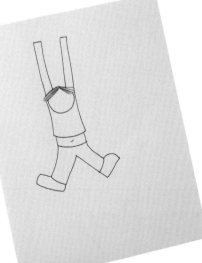

4 Decorate your person and fold the hands over toward the front.

5 Draw and cut out a hat from card stock. Glue it onto the star. Let dry. Hang your person from the middle of the tail.

A shooting star to hang on your door!

Read About

Books

The Bumper Book of Crafty Activities: 100+ Creative Ideas for Kids. Petaluma, Calif.: Search Press, 2012.

Hardy, Emma. *Green Crafts for Children.* New York: Ryland Peters & Small, 2008.

Shields, Amy. *Christmas Unwrapped: A Kid's Winter Wonderland of Holiday Trivia.* New York: Sky Pony Press, 2011.

Internet Addresses

Kaboose: Christmas Crafts
<http://crafts.kaboose.com/holidays/christmas/christmas-crafts.html>

FamilyFun: Christmas Craft Ideas
<http://familyfun.go.com/christmas/christmas-gifts-cards-decorations/>

Index
Easy to Hard